York St John

Libr... ...rmation S...

Stitching

Anthony Neilson

1 0 II IN 2023   WITHDRAWN

D0676478

Published by Methuen Drama

Copyright © 2002 by Anthony Neilson

The author has asserted his moral rights

ISBN 0 413 77293 4

A CIP catalogue record for this book is available at the British Library

Typeset by SX Composing DTP, Rayleigh, Essex
Transferred to digital printing 2002

Caution
All rights whatsoever in this play are strictly reserved. Enquiries about
rights for amateur and professional performances should be directed
to Julia Tyrell, McFarlane Chad, 33 Percy Street, London W1.
No performance may be given unless a licence has been obtained.

This paperback is sold subject to the condition that it shall not, by way of
trade or otherwise, be lent, resold, hired out or otherwise circulated without the
publisher's prior consent in any form of binding or cover other than that in which
it is published and without a similar condition including this condition being
imposed on the subsequent purchaser.

THE BUSH THEATRE
AND THE RED ROOM

PRESENT

STITCHING

written & directed
by anthony neilson

YORK ST. JOHN
COLLEGE LIBRARY

10 September –12 October 2002

**we will fix it.
we will mend it . . .**

Cast

Abby	Selina Boyack
Stu	Phil McKee

Director	Anthony Neilson
Designer	Bob Bailey
Lighting Designer	Chahine Yavroyan
Sound Designer	David Denholm
Deputy Stage Manager	Jacqui Findlay
Set Construction by	Simon Kenny at Souvenir
Lead table sculpted by	Robert Bryce Muir

Press Representation

The Bush: Sarah Mitchell
for The Sarah Mitchell
Partnership 020 7434 1944
The Red Room: Emma
Schad

0207 697 8685

Graphic Design

Emma Cooke
at Chamberlain McAuley
020 8858 5545

Publicity Photographer:	Herbie Knott
Production Photographer:	Sean Patterson

This performance lasts approximately 85 minutes
with no interval.

At The Bush Theatre

Artistic Director	Mike Bradwell
Executive Producer	Fiona Clark
General Manager	Jane Grater
Literary Manager	Nicola Wilson
Literary Assistant	Owen Lewis
Marketing Manager	Olivia Wingate
Development Manager	Kate Mitchell
Production Manager	Pam Vision
Resident Stage Manager	John Everett
Chief Electrician	Matt Kirby
Box Office Supervisor	Michael Wagg
Box Office Staff	Dominique Gerrard
	Janet Kumah
Front of House Duty Managers	Kellie Batchelor
	Caroline Beckman
	Johnny Flynn
	Muzz Khan
	Delores Kumah
	Kate Ryan
Associate Artists	Es Devlin
	Julie-Anne Robinson
*Pearson Writer in Residence	Shelley Silas
	Sheila Lemon
Writer in Residence	Isabel Wright

*This theatre has the support of the Pearson Playwrights' Scheme, sponsored by Pearson plc.

At The Red Room

Artistic Director:	Lisa Goldman
Administrative Director:	Emma Schad

Selina Boyack

Theatre includes: *Four Dogs & A Bone* and *The Big Funk* (The Archers Theatre, Glasgow), *Playing Hide And Seek With Jesus* (Edinburgh Festival), *The Reckless Are Dying Out* (Lyric Studio), *How The Other Half Loves* (The Mill At Sonning), *I'll Show You Mine* (Finborough), 'Viola' in *Twelfth Night* (Arts Council Tour of China, Salisbury Playhouse, Royal Lyceum, Edinburgh), *No Big Deal* and *Someone Waiting* (The Orange Tree), *The Recruiting Officer* and 'Helena' in *A Midsummer Night's Dream* (Royal Lyceum, Edinburgh). Television includes: *Second Sight, This Morning With Richard Not Judy, Peak Practice* and *Kavanagh*. Film includes: *The Stick Up, The Debt Collector, Sweeney Todd, The Tribe, Working From Home* and *A Friend In Need*.

Phil McKee

Theatre includes: *Macbeth* (The Cage Theatre at The Landor Theatre), *The Robbers* and *The Boat Plays* (The Gate Theatre), *Richard III, Napoli Milionaria* and *King Lear* (National Theatre) and *Lady Betty* (Cheek By Jowl - Almeida and National Tour). Television includes: *Band of Brothers, The Bill, Heartbeat, Silent Witness, Crime Traveller, Richard II, Soldier Soldier, The Place of the Dead, Taggart* and *Lovejoy*. Film includes: *George & the Dragon, The Lost Battalion, Joan of Arc, Simon Magus, The Debt Collector* and *The Star*.

Anthony Neilson Writer and Director

Plays Anthony has written and directed include: *Edward Gant's Amazing Feats of Loneliness* (Plymouth Drum); *The Censor* (The Red Room at The Finborough/Royal Court), for which he won the Writers Guild Award 1997, Best Fringe Play and the Time Out Live Award 1997, Best New Play On the Fringe; *The Night Before Christmas* (The Red Room); *Penetrator* (Royal Court Theatre Upstairs/Traverse Theatre/Finborough); *The Year of the Family* (Finborough) and *Normal* (Edinburgh Festival). Films include: *The Debt Collector* and *Deeper Still.* Anthony has also written for radio. Up-coming productions include *The Lying Kind* (The Royal Court).

Bob Bailey Designer

Graduated from Central St Martins in 1993. Previous productions include: *Edward Gant's Amazing Feats of Loneliness* (Plymouth Drum, Dir. Anthony Neilson), *Aeroplane Man* (Stratford East, Dir: Johnzi-D), *La Ronde* (RADA. Dir. Carlos Wagner), *Grapes of Wrath* (Finborough), and *Angels in America* (Crucible Sheffield), both directed by Phil Wilmott, *Blueprint* (Royal Opera House Education, Dir. Joe Davis), *Venezia* (Royal National Theatre Studio/Gate Theatre), *Hijrah* (Plymouth Drum and The Bush Theatre, Dir. Ian Brown). In 1999 Bob was awarded the Time Out Designer of the Year Award for *The Happiest Days of My Life* (DV8 Dance Company, UK and European Tour). Other designs include: *Charley's Aunt* (Sheffield Crucible, Dir. Deborah Paige), *Dancing at Lughnasa* (Jermyn Street, Dir. Gillian King), *Mrs Harris Goes to Paris* (London Children's Ballet, Peacock Theatre, Choreo. Harold King), *Horseplay* and *All Nighter* (both Dancebites for the Royal Ballet, Choreo. Tom Sapsford), *Good Works* and *Rough Music* (Show of Strength, Bristol). Bob was the recipient of an Arts Council Bursary for Stage Design to work at the Bristol Old Vic, where productions included *Beaux Stratagem* (costumes); *Enemy of the People* (costumes); *Moll Flanders* (set/costumes); *Translations* (set/costumes), all directed by Ian Hastings. Bob is currently designing *Tosca* for the Nationale Reisopera, Holland, Dir. Carlos Wagner.

Chahine Yavroyan Lighting Designer

Chahine worked with Anthony Neilson on his last project prior to *Stitching*, *Edward Gant's Amazing Feats of Loneliness* (The Drum, Plymouth). Previously for The Bush Theatre, Chahine has worked on *Whistlestop, Shang-a-lang* and *Darwin's Flood*. Other productions include *Green Field, Gagarin Way, King of the Fields, The Speculator, Perfect Days, Anna Weiss, Knives in Hens* and *The Architect* (Traverse), *South Pacific* and *King Lear* (The Crucible), *Pygmalion* (Nottingham Playhouse), A *Midsummer Night's Dream* and *Macbeth* (Leicester Haymarket), *Hedda Gabler* and *Wolk's World* (The Royal Exchange), *Standing Room Only* and *Tantamount Esperance* (Rose English, 1st Class Evening's Entertainment for Post Operative Productions), *An Die Musik* (Pip Simmons) and *Variete* (Lindsay Kemp). As well as theatre and dance, he has lit objects, clothes, casts of one to 234, back rooms of pubs and main stages, indoors and outdoors.

David Denholm Sound Designer

David Denholm is a composer and lectures in Music Technology at Birmingham Conservatoire, where he is undergoing research into computer-aided composition. His compositions utilise technology which responds to the instrumentalist's performance. He is also Head of Sound at Birmingham School of Speech and Drama and sound designer for many of the school's shows, ranging from Shakespeare to contemporary writing. He currently works in the studio as a producer for new talent.

30 Years of The Bush Theatre

The Bush Theatre opened in April 1972 in the upstairs dining room of The Bush Hotel, Shepherds Bush Green. The room had previously served as Lionel Blair's dance studio. Since then, The Bush has become the country's leading new writing venue with over 350 productions, premiering the finest new writing talent.

Playwrights whose works have been performed here at The Bush include Stephen Poliakoff, Robert Holman, Tina Brown, Snoo Wilson, John Byrne, Ron Hutchinson, Terry Johnson, Beth Henley, Kevin Elyot, Doug Lucie, Dusty Hughes, Sharman McDonald, Billy Roche, Tony Kushner, Catherine Johnson, Philip Ridley, Richard Cameron, Jonathan Harvey, Richard Zajdlic, Naomi Wallace, David Eldridge, Conor McPherson, Joe Penhall, Helen Blakeman, Lucy Gannon, Mark O'Rowe and Charlotte Jones.

The theatre has also attracted major acting and directing talents including Bob Hoskins, Alan Rickman, Antony Sher, Stephen Rea, Frances Barber, Lindsay Duncan, Brian Cox, Kate Beckinsale, Patricia Hodge, Simon Callow, Alison Steadman, Jim Broadbent, Tim Roth, Jane Horrocks, Gwen Taylor, Mike Leigh, Mike Figgis, Mike Newell and Richard Wilson.

Victoria Wood and Julie Walters first worked together at The Bush, and Victoria wrote her first sketch on an old typewriter she found backstage.

In 30 years, The Bush has won over one hundred awards. Bush plays have transferred to the West End and Broadway, and have been successfully adapted for film and television. Bush productions have toured throughout Britain, Europe and North America.

Every year we receive over fifteen hundred scripts through the post, and we read them all. According to The Sunday Times;

"What happens at The Bush today is at the very heart of tomorrow's theatre"

That's why we read all the scripts and will continue to do so for at least another 30 years. We hope you'll be here too.

Mike Bradwell
Artistic Director

Fiona Clark
Executive Producer

The Red Room

The Red Room exists to cut through the complacency of the new writing industry and free the imagination against the status quo. We aim to create work which will provoke and inspire - that is fresh, diverse, radical, honest and brave.

The Red Room was created in 1995 by Lisa Goldman and Emma Schad converting a derelict room above the (then) derelict Lion and Unicorn pub in Kentish Town. Our first season of work contained the premieres of The Shorewatchers House by Judy Upton, The Night before Christmas by Anthony Neilson and Joe Crilly's first play Shuttle. In our first extraordinary year we premiered 12 new plays by new and more established writers. Set budgets were often around 50 quid, wages were non-existent - the success of our enterprise came about through the sheer hard work and inspirational force of the people who joined us. One of these people was Anthony Neilson, who we then commissioned to create the Censor for our Big Story season about the media. In 1997 The Red Room transferred The Censor to the Royal Court Duke of Yorks and it won Writers Guild Award and Time Out Live Award for Best Fringe Play.

Since leaving our first home the Red Room has become a successful production company, curating work prolifically for BAC - three Critics Choice seasons (with Obsession, Surfing and Sunspots) and a two month residency in Studio 1 for which we created the political new writing festival Seeing Red. Seeing Red was the first clearly critical theatrical statement against the New Labour government to take place in London. It slyly asked writers to respond to the thirtieth anniversary of 1968 and the first anniversary of the Labour election victory at a time when dissent was just a whisper. The sixteen writers included Rebecca Prichard, Roddy McDevitt, Peter Barnes, Judy Upton, Parv Bancil, Roney Fraser Munro, Paul Sirett, Tony Craze, David Eldridge and Helen Kelly. Two of the plays became full length commissions which had a successful future life, both developed and directed by Lisa Goldman. Made in England by Parv Bancil had a highly acclaimed tour and The Bogus Woman by Kay Adshead was awarded a Fringe First at the Traverse in 2000, was a sell out success at the Bush theatre and toured nationally and internationally before being made by the same team into a Radio 3 Sunday Play.

The Red Room also involves itself in debates and activism around culture and politics. Most recently the company initiated Artists Against the War - building a network, exhibiting art work, creating work for demonstrations and as a demonstration - most recently Palestine Verbatim in Trafalgar Square, organised with Meeting Ground in June 2002, where actors like Maggie Steed, Harriet Walter, Deborah Findlay and David Calder read testimony, mainly from Palestinians in occupied territories, but also Israeli refuseniks.

This autumn the Red Room is curating a writers lab and performed debate about public theatre. We are also developing new projects, the next of which will be Kay Adshead's Animal, a play which examines human experiment. We are also researching for a new public theatre piece about regeneration, set in east London.

Stitching is a deeply private exploration, which collides with public consciousness in an unsettling way and to which men and women will no doubt have their own very private response. The high risk process of Anthony's work is an important antdote to complacency on every level and we are very pleased that The Bush have collaborated with The Red Room to facilitate this provocative and visceral play of tenderness and brutality - an intimate sexual dialogue between grieving parents set against their earlier decision about whether or not to have the child.

We welcome involvement and participation in The Red Room's work. If you would like to find out more about future projects or are in a position to offer time, resources or financial support we would love to hear from you.

We would like to thank all those that have generously supported our work over the last seven years and gratefully acknowledge our recent receipt of core funding from London Arts and ongoing support from the Arts Council of England.

The Red Room,
Cabin Q,
Clarendon Buildings,
11 Ronald's Road,
London,
N5 1XJ

Tel: 020 7 697 8685
Email: info@theredroom.org.uk
wwww.theredroom.org.uk

COMING SOON to The Bush Theatre

Naked Talent:
A New Playwrights' Festival

The Bush continues its 30th Anniversary Season with the presentation of the NAKED TALENT festival, celebrating new writing by premiering three first full-length plays from some of the sharpest new voices of today's theatre.
PREMIERING:

adrenalin...heart by Georgia Fitch
Directed by Mike Bradwell, Designed by Martin Reynolds
23 OCTOBER - 9 NOVEMBER

"Someone in a white coat said I was one of those who are addicted to the total all embracing experience"

On meeting Angel, Leigh's life is turned upside down. Sex, race, drugs and verbals collide in this terrifying roller-coaster of a drama.

Falling by Shelley Silas
Directed by John Tiffany, Designed by Martin Reynolds
12 - 30 NOVEMBER

"She hates me, apparently I make her sick and she wishes she'd never been born."

Falling is a domestic comedy drama about teenage angst, mid life crisis, babies and sibling rivalry. It's about knowing when to give up, give in and get on with your life. And about growing up and growing old gracefully, even when you are only 40.

Untouchable by Simon Burt
Directed by Natasha Betteridge, Designed by Martin Reynolds
3 - 21 DECEMBER

"Tonight we keep going 'til we watch sun rise over Argos Superstore..."

Louise and Manni are eighteen, bestest friends since forever. They're going to live up town, go clubbing and get off with boys. There's only the one bed but they're sure they can work round that. They're untouchable. Nothing is ever going to come between them. Nothing... except for drink, sex and sleepy wandering hands under the duvet...

Tickets £10.00-13.50 (£7.50-8.75 concessions) plus annual membership £1
SUBSCRIPTION OFFER - 20% off when you buy tickets to all three shows
Book online at www.bushtheatre.co.uk (no booking fee) or call 020 7610 4224

Support The Bush

The Bush Theatre is a writers' theatre. We commission, develop and produce exclusively new plays. In addition to reading every script sent in, we commission up to seven writers each year and offer a bespoke programme of workshops and one-to-one dramaturgy to develop their plays. Our international reputation of 30 years is built on consistently producing the very best work to the very highest standard.

The search for new voices and the quest to reach as wide an audience as possible is ongoing. It is an ever-increasing challenge. We gratefully acknowledge support for our core programme from London Arts and London Borough of Hammersmith and Fulham. However, there are many individuals and companies whose generous support enables us to maintain and expand the programme of writer's development and continue to reach new young voices.

The Bush Theatre is launching a new **Patron Scheme** to coincide with its 30th Birthday season. The new scheme will offer opportunities for both Individual and Corporate Giving. We hope participating patrons will form a close relationship with the theatre in addition to receiving a wide range of benefits, which will include ticket offers and invitations to special events. This new scheme will directly support the Writers' Development Programme and help produce the new writers and new plays of the future.

Please join us in supporting another 30 years of new theatre. For full information on the Patron Scheme, please call Kate Mitchell, Development Manager on 020 7602 3703.

Gold Patrons of The Bush Theatre
The Agency
Giancarla Alen-Buckley
Jim Broadbent
Nick Cave
Joe Conneely
Feelgood Fiction
Ken Griffin
Albert & Lyn Fuss
Jonathan Green
Mary Hoare
ICM
ltnetwork.com
Catherine Johnson
Roy MacGregor
The Mackintosh Foundation
Michael Palin
Ralph Picken
Universal Pictures
6th Floor Ltd
Richard Wilson
William Morris Agency (UK) Ltd
Working Title Films

Patrons of The Bush Theatre
Alan Brodie Representation
Alexandra Cann Representation
Conway, Van Gelder
Gillian Diamond
Paola Dionisotti
Charles Elton
Chloë Emmerson
David and Yvonna Gold
David Hare
Amanda Howard Associates
Philip Jackson
Peter Kelly and Karen Duggan
Primary Stages Theatre, New York
Marmont Management
Tim McInnerny
Stephen Nathan and Colleen Toomey
Samuel French Ltd
Rochelle Stevens & Co
Lady Warner
Richard Warner

The Bush would like to extend special thanks for their support to the following:

The Mathilda and Terrence Kennedy Charitable Trust
The Olivier Foundation

Hammersmith & Fulham
Serving our Community

Stitching

Stitching premiered at the Traverse Theatre, Edinburgh, on
1 August, 2002 and transferred to the Bush Theatre,
London, on 12 September 2002.
The cast was as follows:

Abby　　　Selina Boyack
Stu　　　Phil McKee

Director Anthony Neilson
Designer Bob Bailey
Lighting Designer Chahine Yavroyan
Sound Designer David Denholm

One

A man and a woman, in silence, until . . .

Stu Right.

Pause.

Shall I ask the obvious question?

Pause.

I just want to know what's ruled out.

Pause.

Abby It's not just my decision.

He looks at her, dubious.

Stu No, it's just that you always say it is.

Abby My decision?

Stu The woman's decision. And it is: It's your body and it's your decision and if you say no, that's the bottom line and we know that's not on the table.

She bristles at the formality of the term.

I know it sounds cold but I'm trying to be logical.

Pause.

Abby Is it what you want?

Stu No I just –

Abby Then it's out.

Pause.

Stu Right.

Pause.

It's not something you'd consider.

Abby Is it what you want?

Stu   It's not about what I want – it's about what you want.

Abby   What I want depends on what you want.

Stu   I don't *know* what I want.

In response to her expression:

What?

Abby   Then that's an answer isn't it?

Stu   How is that an answer?
Do *you* know what you want? Because if you know what you want, then tell me and we'll go from there.

Pause.

Do you know what you want?

Pause.

Abby   No.

Stu   All right then! So neither of us know what we want. So maybe if we can figure out what we don't want – then what's left will be . . .

Abby   What we want.

Stu (*nods*)   What we want.

Pause.

Abby   So what do we *not* want?

Pause.

What do *you* not want?

Stu   It's not about what *I* don't want It's about what *you* don't want.

Abby   What I don't want depends on what you don't want.

Stu   I don't *know* what I don't want.

The stupidity of this is not lost on them.

All right, look – there's another question I have to ask you. I don't want to ask it but I just – have to, all right?

Pause.

OK?

Pause. The tiniest nod.

Are you sure it's mine?

Abby   You can go and fuck yourself.

She walks out of the room.
He buries his face in his hands.
Pause.
She comes back in.

Abby   Whose is it if it's not fucking yours?! Why would I be talking to you about it if it's not fucking yours?!

Stu   It's not an unreasonable question . . .

Abby   Fuck you!
I'm not the only one who's done stuff – !

Stu   I'm not saying you are –

Abby   You've fucked around just as much as me – !

Stu   I know! That's not/the point – !

Abby   But I'm the one that gets made to feel like a piece of shit – !

Stu   I'm not trying to make you feel like a piece of shit –

Abby   So why d'you ask me something like that then, if it's not to make me feel like a piece of shit?!

Stu   Because I'm not –

Abby   Because that's how it makes me feel! Like a piece of shit!

Stu   Look – I'm not saying that I haven't done it – I have –

Abby   So why d'you ask me something like that?

Stu   Because you're pregnant!

Abby   Oh well excuse me for having a womb!
I'm not so mad on it myself but I'm fucking stuck with it!

Stu   This is insane. One of us is absolutely insane.

Abby   You!

Stu   Yes. Maybe. I don't know anymore. I really don't.

Pause.

Let's do the paper thing.

Abby   No.

Stu   Come on.

Abby   Why?

Stu   Because we're not getting anywhere like this. It's too –
hectic. Let's do the paper thing. I'll get the stuff, all right?

Pause. He leaves.

She buries her head in her hands.

Stu (*offstage*)   Where's the pens?

Pause.

Abby   Under the phone!

Pause.

(*Shouts.*) Under the phone.

Stu (*offstage*)   Under the phone?

Pause.

He returns, with paper and pens.
He hands her each.

Abby   The pencil?

Sighing heavily, he gives her the pen.

No, it's all right –

Stu   No, it's fine, take the pen

Abby   Isn't there another pen?

Stu   I don't mind the pencil. Really.

Abby   No it's all right, I'll have the pencil.

She keeps the pencil. He sits down.

Stu   Right. You want to start?

She shrugs.

OK, I'll start.

He thinks for a moment then writes. He shakes the pen once or twice, getting the ink to flow.

Stu (*writes:*)   I'm sorry for asking but see it from my point of view. It is possible.

He passes her the piece of paper.

She reads it.

Abby   Oh, fuck – !

Violently, she writes and we know she's just writing fuck you *and she thrusts it at him.*

He doesn't even take it.

Stu   That's not very constructive, is it?

Pause.

Come on.

Pause.

She writes a fuller reply and shows it to him: It's NOT possible because a) it was too long ago and b) unlike YOU, I used protection.

He reads, nods. Writes a reply: Fine – I accept that. That's all I wanted to know.

He hands it to her – then takes it back, to write an addendum: All of our problems come down to communication.

He passes it to her.

Pause.

Abby   What's that say?

Stu   All of our problems come down to communication.

Abby   Oh, this is a lot of shit!

Pause.

Why don't we just go back to Relate?

Stu *sighs heavily.*

Abby   It helped for a while.

Stu   For a while . . .

Abby   No, but we let it slip. You know we did.

Stu   Yes but why?

Pause. She realizes his question is not rhetorical.

Abby   Me?

Stu   We.

Abby   It wasn't me that let it slip.

Stu   What, so it was me?

Abby   To start with, yes; I think it was.

Stu   How was it me?

Abby   I'm not saying I didn't let it slip as well but that's because eventually I gave up trying.

Stu   Which is letting it slip.

Abby (*pause*)   Yes, but . . .

Stu   I mean it doesn't really matter who let it slip first because then the other one has to keep it going and vice versa. That's the whole point. That's how you don't let it slip.

Abby   You can't keep it going by yourself.

Stu   No but I don't think you did have to keep it going by yourself. And I think you did let it slip.

Abby   Me?

Stu   On that occasion, yeah.

Abby   Well that's just crap –

Stu   Well wait a minute don't just say 'that's just crap' –

Abby   I didn't say it like that –

Stu   Yes, you did – 'that's just crap!'

Abby   I didn't go – 'that's just CRAP!'

Stu   Well not like *that*, no –

Abby   I said, 'Well, that's just crap.'

Stu   Bollocks, you did; you went 'that's just CRAP!' And it's not helpful cos it just pisses me off.

Abby   Oh I'm so sorry for pissing you off!

Pause.

Stu   Okay; let's say it *was* me that let it slip, all right? For the sake of argument, it was me that let it slip. It doesn't matter –

Pause.

Abby   Maybe I did let it slip. In some ways I/probably did.

Stu   How come when I say it was me that let it slip, now you're saying it was you?!!

Abby   I'm not saying it was *all* me – !

Stu   No but that's the problem; it's all just attack, defend, attack, defend –

Abby   You do it too!

Stu   I'm not *saying* it's just you! Jesus Fucking Christ!!

Pause.

Abby   I don't want to bring a child up with its parents fighting all the time.

Stu   You think I do? (*Pause.*) Christ, I had years of it.

Abby   No, but I can't. And I won't. Whatever that means.

Pause. He nods.

So we have to work this out and we have to do it now. We have to be honest with ourselves. Agreed?

He shrugs, reluctantly assenting. **Abbey** *sings:*

We will fix it, we will mend it.

Stu   We'll need alcohol.

He leaves. Pause.

Abby (*sings*)   We will fix it, we will mend it . . .

Two

A bedsit.

Stuart *waits.*

Abby *enters, cautiously, hovering at the threshold.*

Pause.

Abby   Nice.

Stu   No. It's not. But there you go.

Pause.

Step inside; you won't catch anything.

She does. Pause. They embrace passionately. He buries his face in her neck. She pushes him away and slaps his face.

Abby   Money first.

Pause.

Stu   Seriously? You want money?

Abby   I said so, didn't I?

Puase. He touches her again.

Stu   You said a lot of things.

She slaps him again, harder.

Fucking hell, that was sore!!

Abby   I'm not joking.

Stu   How much money?

Abby   A hundred.

Stu   A hundred?! And what does that get me?

Abby   Sex.

Stu   Sex?

She nods.

Abby   Intercourse.

Stu   Just intercourse?

She nods.

What about oral sex? Do you do that?

Abby (*shrugs*)   Why not?

Stu   How much is that?

Abby   Um – a hundred and twenty.

Stu   A hundred and twenty? That's more expensive than sex.

Abby   Is that unusual?

Stu   It's usually less for a blowjob than for sex.

Abby   Why?

Stu   Well, because – it's not as big a deal.

Abby   Isn't it?

Stu   It doesn't take as long.

Abby   That's not been my experience.

Stu   No but it's not so intimate, is it?

She considers this.

Stu   The vagina's more intimate than the mouth.

Abby   No, it's not. Inside is inside. It's maybe more *secret*, but it's not more intimate.

Pause.

Stu   So how much for a wank?

Abby   Same price/as for everyone else.

Stu   as for everyone else/yes, OK – How much for a *hand-job*?

Abby   A hundred and fifty.

Stu   A hundred and fifty?! But masturbation's less intimate than straight sex or oral sex!

Abby   It's a lot more effort.

Pause.

Stu   I don't think you've got the hang of this.

Abby   I'm just a student, trying to get by.

Stu   A mature student.

Abby   Yes. A mature student.

Pause.

Stu   Will you take fifty?

Pause.

Abby   OK.

Stu   OK?

She shrugs.

All right.

Pause.

Sit beside me then.

Pause. She sits beside him. He touches her hand. She doesn't respond.

He rests his head on her shoulder. She gets up.

Abby   Please don't do that.

Stu   I'm sorry –

Abby   That's not why I'm here.

Stu   I know. I'm sorry.

Pause.

Abby   This isn't about love. This is just a fuck to me – one fuck in a huge wide ocean of fucks.

Stu   An ocean of fucks; I'm with you, absolutely.

Pause.

So let's do it.

Abby   Money first.

He searches his pockets.

Stu   I'll have to go to a hole in the wall.

Abby   It won't make you feel like I will.

Pause.

Stu   Will you trust me for it?

Abby   Why would I do that? I don't even know you.

Stu   I've got the money. I'll get it for you when you leave.

Abby   I'm leaving now.

She starts to go.

Stu   No, wait –

He searches in his pockets again, drags out some notes.

I've got about – thirty pounds or so.

Abby   That's not enough.

Pause.

Watch.

She points at his wrist.

Stu   You want my watch?

Abby   For security.

Stu   It's not worth anything. Not money, anyway. (*Pause.*) It was my father's watch. (*Pause.*) He died.

Pause.

Abby   I'm sorry.

He nods. Pause.

Stu   He had a/heart attack.

Abby   Don't tell me. I don't care.

Pause.

When you pay me, you'll get it back.

Pause. He nods, taking it off and giving it to her.

She looks at it.

Stu   What?

Abby   Four forty-four.

Stu   What did you think it was?

Pause.

Abby   No, it's just – everytime I look at a clock, it's always a time with the same numbers: three thirty-three, or four forty-four, or eleven-eleven. Mostly eleven-eleven.

Pause.

Stu   What do you think it means?

Abby   Nothing. What would it mean?

He shrugs.

Abby   Nothing.

She puts the watch in her bag.

So what do you want? Sex?

Stu   Guess so.

She takes off her jacket and fishes in her bag.

Condoms.

Abby   Of course.

Stu   You're well prepared.

Abby   All students carry condoms.

Pause.

Stu   Should we go to the bedroom?

Abby   Wherever you like.

Pause. He walks into the bedroom. She follows.

Music.

The light moves in the empty room, as clouds pass across the sun.

Stuart returns, doing up his trousers. He sits down and lights a cigarette.

Abby *arrives in the doorway, doing up her blouse.*

Pause.

Abby   Well? Shall we go?

He nods. Pause.

Stu   I remember when I was a kid –

Abby   Look, don't fucking bother OK? I know you just came but I don't need you getting all reflective on me.

Stu   It's not sentimental –

Abby   I don't care. I don't give a shit what you remember. All I want is the money you owe me.

Pause.

Stu   I'll pay you to stay. I'll pay you to listen.

Abby   You couldn't afford it.

He nods. Pause.

He puts his coat on. She watches him.

Abby *(V/O)*
Will this be a memory?
Do we feel them as they form?
How do we know which moments will take root in us?
Maybe I'll never have another.
Maybe memories are all behind me.

Stu   Right then.

Snapped from her trance, she checks in her bag for her keys.

Stu   The moment I put this money in your hand, you'll be a whore. You know that, don't you? There's no other word for it. You'll be a whore.

Her keys are there.

Abby   And if I don't take it? What will I be then?

Stu   Just a woman. Just a woman who met a man and had sex with him.

Pause.

Abby   I think I'll take the money please.

Pause.

Stu   So if you're a whore, I can hire you again; can't I?

Pause.

What about Sunday?

Abby   Sunday's the Lord's day.

Pause.

Stu   Fuck him.

Fade to black

Three

Stu (*offstage*)   Where's the corkscrew?

Abby   Isn't it in the drawer?

Stu (*offstage*)   No, obviously not . . .

Abby   It was there this morning . . .

Pause. He enters, carrying a bottle of wine, two glasses and the corkscrew. He gets on with uncorking the wine.

Abby   Where was it?

He pretends not to hear.

Stu   What?

Abby   The corkscrew.

Stu (*grumbling*)   Right at the fucking back . . .

Abby   Right at the fucking back of the drawer?

He ignores her baiting. He hands her a glass of wine.

Stu   Well?

Abby   Well what?

Stu   I don't know. Congratulations, I guess.

Abby   Congratulations.

Stu   Well, it means we're fertile, doesn't it?

Abby   I never doubted that we were.

Stu   I did.

Abby   I know. That's why I'm pregnant.

Pause. She touches her glass to his.

To fertility.

They drink. Pause.

Of course I never meant to fall for you.

Stu   So you keep saying.

Abby   You know what did it?

Stu   My stunning physique?

Abby   No, it was a dream I had.

Stu   A dream?

Abby   Did I never tell you this?

Pause.

Stu   Don't think so.

Abby   It's stupid, really. I had a dream we were living with each other. And in the dream, we loved each other; and it felt all right, it felt good. And then, when I woke up – all of a sudden, I did.

Stu   Did what?

Abby   Loved you. (*Pause.*) All right, not loved you, not right away, but I felt close to you; and suddenly it was a possibility that I could.

Pause.

Is that bad?

Stu   What, that our entire relationship is based on a dream?

Abby   Not based on it. If you'd turned out to be a total cunt, I wouldn't have stuck with it because of the dream.

Stu   I thought I did turn out to be a total cunt.

Abby   Did you?

Stu   I don't know. That's just what I took from you calling me a total cunt.

Abby   When did I call you a total cunt?

Stu   What day is it?

Abby   Tuesday.

Stu   Monday.

Abby   Yes, well, on Monday, you were a total cunt.

Pause.

Stu   So if you hadn't had this dream . . . ?

Abby   Oh I wish I hadn't told you now!

Stu   I'm glad you did.

Abby   It's not a big deal.

Stu   No: just a bit disturbing to find out our whole relationship's based on a dream.

She sighs. Pause.

Abby   Anyway, they're all based on a dream. The house, the kids, the dog; the happily-ever-after. That's what hurts when you lose them. That's what you lose; the little dream you had.

Stu You lose the person.

Abby No you don't.

Stu It's losing the person that hurts, not some dream.

Abby No, because you don't lose the person. If we split up, you won't lose *me*. I'll still be around. What you'd lose is – our possible future.

Pause.

Stu Is that what we're talking about here? That if we don't have this child, it's over?

Abby What would be the point in going on?

Stu See, it's you that'd lose a dream or a future, not me. Cos I don't think this is about whether we have a kid, *full stop*. This is just about whether we have a kid right now.

Abby No it isn't. You know it isn't.

Stu Do I?

Abby Yes because I don't have the *time* to fuck around, Stuart –

Stu Didn't stop you before.

Pause.

Abby Do you want to go down that road? Do you? Do you really want to go down that road?

Stu No –

Abby Because I can go down that road if you want.

Stu No, I don't, I'm sorry. I don't want to go down that road.
I'm sorry. I understand what you're saying about not having time but I just think you're exaggerating.

Abby   Don't tell me I'm exaggerating! I know how I feel.

Stu   You're only thirty . . .

Abby   Yes and so I hang around for *another* four years waiting for you, do I? What happens then? Then I have to find someone else and then when I've found them, I have to figure out whether I want to have kids with them and then bang, I'm forty!

Stu   Oooh, *forty*!

Abby   Well maybe I want to have more than one kid. And it takes a lot of energy to bring up children – it's *tiring* – !

Stu   You're assuming in four years I'd say no but maybe I wouldn't; we'd be a bit more settled, have our careers sorted out –

Abby   No, fuck off, no: we don't have this child, that's it for us.

The enormity of what she's said hangs in the air, shocking even her.

I would hold it against you. I know I would.

Stu   That's blackmail.

Abby   Call it what you want but that's it, it has to be. For me, it does, and that's just it.

Pause. She leaves. He pours himself another drink.

Stu (*V/O*)

Is it you, then?
Is yours the last mouth I'll ever kiss, the last cunt I'll ever touch, the last nipple I'll suck?
Are you all that stands between me and the grave? Am I wrong to feel fear; am I weak, am I shallow?
Does it mean that I don't love you?
Do you not feel it too?

Pause.

Four

Abby *comes in, hangs up her jacket.*

Stu   You're late.

Abby   I know.

Stu   Is that a sorry?

Abby   I'm not sorry. I'm just late.

Pause.

Stu   Why are you late?

Abby   No reason, I'm just late.

Pause.

Stu   You've never been late before.

Abby   So why are you giving me a hard time about it?

Stu   I'm not, I just – I'm not.

Pause.

Abby   Are you drunk?

Stu   No, I'm not drunk, I've just been – drinking. Would you care to join me?

He offers her the bottle. Pause.
She takes a long swig from it, hands it back.

Stu   Oh, I like *you*. You're *fun*.

Pause.

Stu   How's college?

Abby   It's an education.

He waves some money at her. Smiling, she comes to him.

He feigns puzzlement.

Abby   What?

Stu   What's that in your mouth?

Abby   Where?

Stu   Open your mouth.

She opens her mouth. He stuffs the money in. She spits it out.

Abby   You prick. You don't know where that's been.

Stu   Yes I do. William Hill's.

She takes another drink.

I've got something else for you. A present.

Abby   I don't want any/presents.

Stu   Some stuff I thought might help you in your new career.

He hands her a folder, full of sheets of paper.

She leafs through it. It's pornography, downloaded from the internet.

It's a wonderful thing, the internet, don't you think?
I mean, when I was a kid, we had to hope we'd find some hidden in a bush somewhere. Now it's all right there; all the perversions known to man, right at your fingertips. You name it, someone's out there fucking it and sticking pictures of it on the web.

Abby   Is this supposed to shock me?

Stu   No, not at all. I just think – you know – no offence but you're still an amateur. These are the professionals here –

She throws them aside.

I know; you're not a whore. You're just a poor mature student, trying to get by.

Abby   Whatever I am, I'm not a porn star.

He picks them up.

Stu   No but it's the same skill – it's knowing what men want –

Abby   I know what men want.

Stu   I don't think you do. I mean, look at you.

Abby   What?

Stu   The shoes for a start.

Abby   What's wrong with them?

Stu   Well, I'm sure they're very attractive to *students* but if you're serious about your work, it's got to be heels. Stilettos, boots – anything that gives a nice long line to the leg. You know why? Because a girl's legs get longer just as she reaches sexual maturity. So long legs mean youthfulness and . . . don't you get all this in psychology?

Pause.

They also affect your posture, pushing the tits out and pulling the arse in. Talking of which, you're too fucking skinny; what do you eat?

Abby   Cum, mostly. And sometimes Ryvita.

Stu   Eat more fats and carbohydrates, get some meat on you. Skirts of course – never trousers – are you listening to me?

Abby   Yes, sir. I've got a leather skirt, sir, if that'll do.

Stu   No, it has to be something more school-girly.

Abby   Men want to fuck schoolgirls. What a revelation.

Stu   No we don't want to fuck schoolgirls. We want to fuck women dressed like schoolgirls. Because we remember them fondly –we remember their little thighs, and the foundation on their collars and their embarrassed little nipples in their swimsuits . . .

Abby   *Sounds* like you want to fuck them.

Stu   Yes, but it's illegal; so you will have to do. So you must also wear socks – up to the thighs is best –

Abby   Those are stockings.

Stu   Yes –

Abby   Schoolgirls don't wear stockings.

Stu   No, OK – well, knee length is good too. They're all good. All socks and footwear are good. Make-up too. You have to wear make-up.

Abby   I am wearing make-up.

Stu   Yes, but lipstick –

Abby   I'm wearing lipstick!

She shows him. Pause.

Stu   OK, but it's too subtle. Lipstick should be bright red, cos it's your vagina –

Abby   Oh, that's shit.

Stu   'That's shit,' is it?

Abby   I'm not trying to make my mouth look like my cunt.

Stu   Anyway, that's not the point; I'm telling you what men want and they want moist, shiny, bright red lips –

Abby   My cunt's not bright red: What am I, a baboon?

Stu   Garter belts, corsets, you can't go wrong with that. Colour's important, too; personally, I don't like primary colours. Black is good but best of all is white because it's . . . clean and –

Pause.

Abby   Virginal.

Pause.

Stu   I'm sorry.

Pause.

Undressing: all undressing must be done slowly, especially taking off your knickers. This should be done with your back arched, so your arse is prominent and pointed at me. Only small knickers should be worn, no big nursey pants. The thumbs should be hooked under the waistbands and slid slowly down, in one smooth gesture, revealing your cuntlips at the same time.

Abby   *Jawohl, mein Kapitan!*

Stu   Kissing –

Abby   I don't kiss.

Stu   Neither do they, not properly. Because kissing doesn't film well. You can't see what's going on and you've got to remember that men are visual. They like to see. So what they do is they lick each other's tongues. Stick your tongue out.

She sticks her tongue out. At him.

Stu   No, properly. Come here.

Abby   They lick each other's tongues, I get it.

Stu   No, but come here.

Abby   Why?

Stu   Don't you want to be good at what you do?

Abby   Aren't I good enough?

Stu   Good enough's not good enough.

Abby   It's a free market. Shop around.

He grabs hold of her hair.

Stu   Don't tell me to shop around! If I have to pay you like a whore, then that's what I want; the whore of all my dreams, the mother of all fucking whores, not some cunt in comfortable shoes!

Abby   Let go of my hair.

Pause. He lets go.

Pause. She steps back to him, and replaces his hand at the back of her head.

Abby   Do it again.

He bunches her hair in his hand.

Harder.

He twists further and her face contorts in pain.

Stu   D'you like that, do you?

He twists even more.

D'you like that, you fucking whore?

They sink to their knees.

Abby   Tell me what you're going to make me do.

Stu   We're not going to fuck any more. We're not going to use any condoms.
You're going to suck my cock. And lick my balls.
And you're going to look at me while you do it.

Abby   Yes.

Stu   You're going to suck my cock like your life depends on it.

Abby   Yes.

Stu   And you're going to open your mouth and stick out your tongue and you're going to beg me to come in your mouth –
And then I'm going to come right down your throat and you're going to swallow it and dribble it, like the whore you are.
Aren't you?

Abby   Yes.

Stu   And then if I need a piss, I'm going to piss on you, on your face and on your tits and you're going to swallow that too, aren't you?

He shakes the pictures out of the folder.

You want to be a whore? I'll show you what whores do.

He finds a picture, shows it to her.

Think you could do that? Think you could suck off a horse? Think you could get a horse's cock up you?

He shows her another.

Look at that – think you could do that? Think you could eat the shit out another woman's arse? Is that shocking enough for you?

He shows her another.

Think you could stick a bottle up your arse? Or this; think you could do this?

He pulls a crumpled piece of paper from his pocket and shows it to her. From this, she recoils.

Abby   Stop!

Pause. He lets go of her. She slides away from him. Pause.

Abby   Why did you show me that?

Pause.

That how you spend your time, is it? Downloading pictures of women mutilating themselves?

Stu   Found your limits, have we?

She picks up the picture again, looks at it.

Abby   Why did you show me that? Is that what turns you on? A woman sewing up her cunt?

She throws it at him. Pause.

I hope not. For your sake.

Stu   I'm sure she got paid for it.

Pause.

Abby   Nobody's forcing you to do this. You don't want to pay me, that's fine. I'll walk away. You feel sad and inadequate, fine. I'll walk away.

You're too tight to pay me, fine. I'll walk away.

Pause.

Just say the word and I'll walk away.

Pause.

Just say the word. Just say the word.

Stu   Walk away then.

Pause.

Abby   Fine.

She goes to the door: but stops there.

Stu   No. Don't.

He doesn't see, but she is relieved.

Pause.

The first time I came, you know what I was looking at? A book about Auschwitz. All these naked women in a line, waiting to go into a gas chamber. I remember thinking how hairy their cunts were.

Five

Music plays: an overblown power ballad.
The music goes off.

Stu   Abby?!

She re-enters.

Why did you do that?

Abby   Because it's shit.

She picks up the notebook and pen.

Okay: advantages of having a kid, disadvantages of having a kid.

She draws a line down the centre of the page.

Disadvantages . . . relationship a disaster. What else?

Pause.

Stu   Lack of spontaneity.

Abby   Spontaneity?

Stu   Yeah, I mean you can't just get up and bugger off out when you feel like it; got to get babysitters and all that nonsense.

Abby   But when do we do that anyway?

Stu   Yes but we could if we wanted to.

Abby   Right, so we wouldn't be able to do anything spontaneous even though we never do anything spontaneous?

Stu   And there's the cost of it; babysitters, nannies. So we couldn't afford to do anything spontaneous even if we wanted to. Or could.

Abby   Well that makes sense.

Stu   So that's another disadvantage – the cost of it all; prams and clothes and nappies . . .

Abby   We're both working.

Stu   But we wouldn't be, would we?
We couldn't both work, not at first.

Abby   I'm sure we could figure something out.

Stu   I can't take time off, Abby. Not just now.

Abby   Not just *now* . . .

Stu   Not in the next year; you know I can't. If I fuck up this contract, that's going to do none of us any good, is it?

Abby   Right, so basically what you're saying is that you don't want to have this child; so why don't you just say that?

Stu   I'm not saying I don't want to have it . . .

Abby   Well all you can come up with are negatives, I mean – can you not think of a single advantage to having it?

Stu   Of course I can think of advantages . . .

Abby   So come on then – just give me one.

Pause.

Stu   There's lots of advantages –

Abby   Like what?

Stu   Like just – having a kid; having something that you love and that loves you back, it'd be – nice.

Abby   Nice.

Stu   Lovely. Wonderful. Amazing. All right? That's not the issue; it's whether we're ready for it now.

Abby   Whether we'll ever be ready for it.

Stu   Isn't that what we're trying to work out?

She turns back to another page.

Abby   Yes – Where We Went Wrong: Missed out on courting, stroke, had sex too soon. You weren't over girlfriend, stroke, too fucked up for relationship –

Stu   Look, we can go back over all that but you know what the problem is; the problem is all the betrayals, all the infidelities, right from the word go . . .

Pause.

Basically, we've got to clean the slate. Forget the past. Start again. Maybe having a kid would force us to do that.

Abby   It'd have to.

Pause.

Stu   OK, let's be positive. We could work it out. We could get a nanny and I could take *some* time off; just not much. People do it; just a question of time management.

Abby   That's rich coming from you.

Stu   How?

Abby   The closest you get to time management is pissing in the sink while you brush your teeth.

[This section should be improvised to suit the actors.]

Stu   Says the woman with the potty under the bed.

Abby   Says the man with the stupid fucking Star-Trek figures.

Stu   Says the woman who used to fancy Bamber Gascoigne.

Abby   Says the man who fancies Tina from S Club 7.

Stu   Says the woman who leaves a father's shit smell in the toilet and tries to cover it up with hairspray –

Exclaiming, she jumps on him.

Abby   Says the hairy fucking ginger-boy Scottish fucking – twat!!

They roll around on the floor, her trying to tickle him, and both of them shouting things such as these:

Stu   Grey pubes! Bamber Gascoigne! Father's shit!!

Abby   Ginger pubes!! Spotty cock!! Star-Trek boy!!

Music overwhelms them and then the lights change . . .

Six

. . . And now they are rolling on the floor, but this time in the throes of violent sexual passion.
They come apart, breathing heavily. Pause.
He opens a box and takes out a dildo. He forces her to suck it, pushing her head back and forward on it.
It gets too violent and she gags. She pulls his arm away and wrestles the dildo from him.
She sticks it in his mouth and makes him suck it, doing the same to him as he did to her.
After a while, he pushes her down onto the ground, straddling her.
He twists on her nipples. She grabs his ears and twists them. For both of them, the pain gets too much and they come apart.
Pause.
He tries to get her jeans off but she kicks him away. They can hardly speak for the lack of breath.

Stu   I want to shave your cunt.

Abby   Fuck off.

Stu   Please.

Abby   Why?

Stu   So I can see your clit better.

Abby   Are you sure?

Stu   What do you mean?

Abby   Maybe you feel insecure with a woman. Maybe you want me like a girl. Maybe you're a paedophile.

Stu   Maybe. What's it to you?

Abby   And what then?

Stu   What when?

Abby   After I've shaved my cunt. Where do we go then?

Stu   Will you do it?

Pause.

Abby ˙ Two hundred.

Stu Deal.

Abby Show me the money.

Stu I can write you a cheque.

Abby It'll bounce.

Stu It won't; I promise it won't.

Abby Give me the cheque and when it clears, I'll do it.

Stu It'll clear, I promise –

Abby I'll do it for next time.

Stu No but I want to do it.

Abby Think I'm letting you near my cunt with a razor?

Pause.

Stu What do you mean by that?

Pause.

You think I'd hurt you? You think I'd ever do anything to hurt you?

Pause.

Abby I'd like you to. I'd like you to hurt me. I'd like you to drag a razor down my face and throat and tits –

Stu Don't say things like that.

Abby I'd like you to stick a shotgun up my cunt and pull the trigger.

Stu Don't be so fucking stupid!

He gets up, truly shocked.
She gets up and pursues him.

Abby   You know what else I'd like? I'd like us to hurt
someone together.
I'd like us to abduct a child and fuck it and burn it and kill
it.
We could be like the next Moors Murderers or like Fred and
Rosemary West –

Stu   Yes, right, very shocking, very good –

Abby   You know what else I'd like?

Stu   Some valium?

Abby   I'd like to see you seduce the mothers of those
murdered children –

Stu   Abby, shut up –

Abby   I'd like to see you console them and care for them
and win them over.
And then you could bring them back here –

Stu   Abby, shut the fuck up –

Abby   – and I could hide in the cupboard and film you
fucking them and fingering their arseholes and then we
could put the films on the web and sell them –

He covers her mouth.

Stu   Abby, you're talking fucking shite! Why are you being
like this? What are you trying to achieve? Why are you
talking such utter fucking shite?!!

She bites his hand; with a yelp he withdraws it.

Stu   You fucking little cow!

Abby   Don't tell me I'm talking shite.

Pause.

Stu   Look – I don't want to keep playing this game. It was
fun at first but now it's getting boring.

Abby   You don't look bored.

Stu   Well I am. I'm bored of playing out your stupid fantasy.
I'm bored of pretending I don't feel anything for you when I do. I'm bored of pretending what happened/didn't –
(happen)

She slaps him again, ferociously. Pause.

I'm bored of being slapped by you.

Abby   You ever want to see me again, you keep your fucking thoughts to yourself!

She puts her coat on.

Stu   Abby, wait –

She leaves. Pause. He follows.

Abby!

Seven

Stuart *sleepwalks on. He's grinning, but the grin is fixed and false.*
Abby *enters.*

Abby   Stuart? What are you doing up?

Pause.

Come back to bed.

Stu   I can't. It's Daniel's time now.

Pause.

Abby   What do you mean?

Stu   Eleven-eleven.

Abby   Is he here?

Pause.

Stuart, is he here?!

Stu   He's outside by the fire escape.

Abby   No, but – how can that be? I thought he was dead?

Stu   No, no.

Abby   Yes but we dropped him.

Stu   No, no, that was all a mistake. He's fine now.
As long as it's all stitched up, he can stay.

Abby   Stitched up?

Stu   We can do that, can't we?

Pause.

Abby   Yes, of course. That's fine – Where is he?

Stu   He's with your mother, by the oven. But don't look at
his tiddler.

Pause.

Abby   Why not?

Stu   I don't know. It's different somehow.

Abby   Oh. (*Pause.*) OK.

Stu   Are you happy?

Abby   Oh God yes! Yes, of course I am! Oh thank God!!

Stu   Congratulations.

Abby   Thanks.

Pause.

Daniel? Come to Mummy, baby. Come and see Mummy,
my angel. We can go on the choo-choo. We can go on the
choo-choo to the beach.

Eight

Stuart *is shouting down a phone.*

Stu   HELLO?!! HELLO?!!

Pause.

PICK UP THE PHONE!! PICK UP THE FUCKING
PHONE!!

Abby *enters, clutching a questionnaire. She watches him.*

PICK UP THE FUCKING PHONE!!

Abby   Just leave it. They'll notice eventually.

Stu   Who is it, though? Can you hear anything?

He hands her the phone. She listens.

Abby   It's someone walking. In the street; I can hear cars.
It's in someone's bag.

He takes the phone back.

Stu   HELLO?!! PICK UP THE PHONE!!!

Abby   You're going to burst a blood vessel. Just put it
down.

Stu   But how does it happen?

Abby   Someone's dialled us by mistake. It's them that'll
have to pay for it.

Stu   I should fucking hope so.

Abby   Do you want to do this thing?

Pause. He nods.

All right.
When you and your partner disagree, is it more important
to you to
a) find a mutually agreeable solution, or
b) get your own way?

Stu *nods. Pause.*

Abby   Which?

Stu   'a'.

Abby   'a'? (*Pause.*) Find a mutually agreeable solution?

Stu   What about you?

Abby   Well I'd say 'a' as well.

He nods, amused.

Abby   What?

Stu   Nothing.

Abby   You think I try to get my own way?

Stu   Well this is what I mean; there's no point in giving our own answers. I should answer for you and you should answer for me.

Abby   So we'll just have the same problem in reverse.

Stu   No, I'll put what I honestly think.

Abby   I've put what I honestly think. I honestly think that it's more important for me to find a mutually agreeable solution.

Stu   Well, so do I. So both of us think it's more important to find a mutually agreeable solution. So how come we never find a mutually agreeable solution?

Abby   So if you were answering for me, you'd put 'b', that I'd rather get my own way?

Stu   Well what would you put for me?

Abby   For you? I'd . . . probably put 'a'.

Stu   You'd put 'a'?! For me?

Abby   Probably.

Stu   What utter shite!!

Abby   Oh yes, right, cos everything I say is utter fucking SHITE, isn't it??!

Stu   I didn't say utter FUCKING shite –

Abby   That's your idea of finding a mutually agreeable solution is it? To say I'm talking utter fucking SHITE?!

Stu   I just really doubt that you'd put 'a', if you were answering for me.

Abby   No, cos I think it probably *is* more important to you to find a mutually agreeable solution –

Stu   Of course you do.

Abby   – No but I just don't think you find it, and then I end up giving in and you end up getting your own way –

Stu   Fine well let's just – agree to disagree, shall we? Move on.

Abby   Don't tell me to move on.

Stu   Ask the next question.

Pause. She shakes her head. Pause.

Abby   So are we writing answers for each other or for ourselves?

Stu *shrugs.*

All right, we'll answer for each other.

Stu   No, let's do it your way.

Abby   No, it's fine.

Stu   No, I wouldn't want you saying that I always get my own way.

Abby   Oh don't be so fucking petty!!

Stu   I'm not being petty; that's what I'm trying to avoid.

Pause.

Abby   When you are responsible for a problem in your relationship are you quicker to a) get defensive, or b) apologize?

Pause.

Stu   'a'.

Abby   Get defensive.

Stu   Well you *do* – !

Abby   Fine. When your *partner* is responsible for a problem in your relationship –

Stu   Wait a minute – what did you put for me?

Abby   'a'. When your *partner* is responsible for a problem in your relationship – do you find it easier to a) blame, or b) forgive?

Pause.

Stu   I'd really dearly love to put 'b' –

Abby   Oh don't fucking bother – If I found it so fucking hard to forgive then I wouldn't be sitting here now, would I?

Stu   I'm not saying it's any different for me –

Abby   No but some of us have had a bit more to forgive, haven't we?

Stu   Well that's the way you see it –

Abby   You fucked my cousin! I think anyone would see it that way, don't you?

Stu   I didn't *fuck* her –

Abby   Funny cos that's not the way she sees it either. Seems like there's an awful lot of people don't see things the way you do.

Pause.

What stands out more strongly in your mind?
a) what your partner has done right? or b) what your
partner has done wrong?

Pause. They look at each other.
She puts the paper down.

This is pointless.

Pause.

We can't have a child together. Christ, we can barely get
through this stupid fucking *quiz* together.

Long pause.

Stu   I do love you, Abby.

Abby   And I love you. But it's not enough, is it? It should
be but it's not.

Pause.

Stu   We just need a bit of time; to heal ourselves.

Abby   But we don't trust each other, Stuart. There's not
one single shred of trust left between us and we're both to
blame, we're both to blame – but I don't know how you
heal that. How do we heal that?

Pause.

Stu   I don't know either.

Pause.

Abby   Then that's it, isn't it? Nothing more to be said.

Pause.

Stu   You won't have the kid?

Abby   I don't want to be a single mother. I couldn't bear
to have it adopted. So no – I won't have it.

Pause.

I'll have to find somewhere to live.

Tel: 01604 876700

Ready for pickup: 0
Hold requests: 0
Overdue: 0
Checked out: 4
31/10/2017 15:30
Total items: 4

Due: 28/11/2017 23:59
ID: 38052007693796
Title: Passion play

Due: 28/11/2017 23:59
ID: 38052002231139
Title: Stitching

Due: 28/11/2017 23:59
ID: 38052004143944
Title: Dealer's choice

Due: 28/11/2017 23:59
ID: 38052004969272
Title: Leaves of glass

Customer name: SOPHIE PAIGE LILLIELAIR

Check-Out Receipt
York St John University

York St John University
Check-Out Receipt

Customer name: SOPHIE PAIGE LITTLEFAIR

Title: Leaves of glass
ID: 38025004965375
Due: 28/11/2017 23:59

Title: Dealer's choice
ID: 38025004143494
Due: 28/11/2017 23:59

Title: Stitching
ID: 38025005537736
Due: 28/11/2017 23:59

Title: Passion play
ID: 38025001763476
Due: 28/11/2017 23:59

Total items: 4
31/10/2017 15:30
Checked out: 4
Overdue: 0
Hold requests: 0
Ready for pickup: 0

Tel: 01904 876700

They live with the thought for a time.

Stu   No, you can stay here. I'll go.

She nods. Pause.

Abby   Thanks.

Pause. She leaves.

Nine

Abby *sits there, in the bedsit. She is wearing a short skirt and heels.* **Stuart** *enters. He hangs in the doorway, looking at her.*

Abby   Hello Stuart.

Pause.

Stu   Hi.

Pause.

Abby   I hope you don't mind. I let myself in.

Pause.

Stu   Where have you been?

Abby   Around.

Pause.

Stu   Not at college.

Abby   How do you know?

Stu   Because I called them.

Abby   Why did you do that?

Stu   Why did I do that? Well, let me think: we have an argument, you go mental. You tell me if I ever want to see you again, I should keep my fucking thoughts to myself. You storm off out the flat and I don't see or hear from you for three weeks. Oh, yes, I remember: I was worried fucking *sick*.

Abby You didn't need to worry. I'm fine. Better than I've been in a long time.

Stu I'm happy for you.

Abby Thanks.

Pause.

What time is it?

Stu About eleven.

Abby No, *exactly*.

Stu Three . . . four minutes past. Why?

Pause.

Abby When I was a little girl, I got the chicken pox and Dad brought me a present. It was a shitty little plastic brush and I hated it. I was ill and I hated it and when he gave it to me, I threw it across the room.

Pause.

And the only thing I regret more than that is killing Daniel.

Stu We didn't kill him.

Abby We didn't save him, though, did we? We were too busy fighting to hear him die.

Stu Children fall. How many times did you fall as a child?

Pause.

We were unlucky.

Abby But we grew up, didn't we? We went to dinner. We kissed at the bus-stop. We made love.

Pause.

Stu   He wouldn't want this, Abby. He loved us and he knows that we loved him. He'd want us to be together.

Abby   Well – here we are.

Stu   Not like this. Not this game; pretending to be strangers, pretending he never existed – never lived, never died. It's not right.

Pause.

I know you're scared. Of the past, of the future. So am I. We thought losing Daniel would break the link between us. But then I saw you again; and all the time we spent apart just vanished, like it was just some terrible dream. And I realized; of course it hadn't. How could it? All it'd done was lock us together, even tighter than before.
And suddenly – for the first time in God-fucking-knows how long – I suddenly knew where I was going.
And if you had to pretend to be a whore and I had to pretend to be your client – if that was the game you needed to play so you could cope with that, then fine – for a while. But now we have to go forward. We have to be something new. We can't be what we're not. And we can't be what we were.

Abby   Can't we?

Stu   No. We can't.

Pause.

Abby   Do you like my new outfit?

Pause.

Stu   I don't know if I do.

Abby   But it's what you wanted, isn't it?

Pause.

What about the skirt? Isn't it school-girly enough? It's white, like you wanted. All clean and virginal. That's what men want, isn't it? Virginal.

Pause.

Stu   Maybe they just like the idea of it.

Abby   Yes; the idea of it. I know. So they can be special. So you can be special again. So we can be what we were. So Daniel can stay; like you said in the dream.

Stu   Like I said – in the dream?

Abby   That's why I did it.

Stu   Did what?

Abby   You know – what you wanted me to do.

She points at her vagina. Pause. He twigs.

Stu   Oh – that. I wasn't being serious . . . Anyway, you were right: the cheque would've bounced.

Abby   No but I wanted to do it. I've been thinking about it a lot. It's been growing in my head like a seed.

Pause.

Do you want to see?

Pause.

Stu   Maybe later.

Abby   No but I did it for you. Just have a look.

Pause. He nods, kneels down in front of her.

No, wait –

She holds his wrist, staring at his watch.

OK.

She turns to face him and raises her skirt. He looks between her legs.

Pause.

Stu   What's that?

Abby   Touch it.

He does. Pause.

Stu   Is that stubble?

He removes his fingers. They're bloody.

Abby   All stitched up like new. Now he can stay.

He looks again, then recoils in shock.

Stu   Oh my God – Abby, what have you done . . .

Abby (*sings*)   We will fix it, we will mend it . . .

Stu   Oh no – oh Jesus God – what have you done to yourself?!!

Abby (*sings*)   We will fix it, we will mend it . . .

He drops to his knees in horror. He hugs her.

Stu   Oh my baby – my baby – what have you gone and done?

Ten

Stu   The last time I saw her was the next winter.
Ironically enough, I was out buying a present for my then-girlfriend.
Abby was staring into a shop window, her face lit up by the Christmas lights. We went for a cup of coffee.
She looked healthy. She'd put on weight, though she said that was a side-effect. She had a part-time job in a florist's and secure accommodation. She said she could get me a reduction on flowers anytime I wanted.
She said that God loved us, and that Daniel was with him. She said that he was happy there and that he forgave us our selfishness.
Daniel. Danny. Our child. (*Pause.*) My son.
Anyway, we told each other we'd keep in touch and me, I meant it. But there was something funny in the way she said goodbye.

Don't say it like that, I said.
Like what? she said.
'Goodbye, Stuart' like it's goodbye for ever.
I didn't say it like that, she said.
You did, I said.
I didn't.
Yes, I said.
You did.

Eleven

Abby *rejoins him on stage.*

Stu   So that's it, then?

Abby   I guess so.

Stu   So this is what that's-it feels like.

Pause.

Does it feel like that's-it to you?

Abby   I don't know. I don't remember what that's-it feels like.

Pause.

Stu   Doesn't feel very nice, whatever it is.

Abby   No.

Abby   You'll be all right. Men are always all right.

Stu   What do you mean by that?

Abby   Men get over break-ups quicker.

Stu   That's bollocks.

Abby   They do.

Stu   No, people always say that but it's not true; you know why?

Abby   Why?

Stu   Masturbation.

Abby   Of course.

Stu   No, seriously; it's actually the male that carries regret the longest. Because the need to masturbate forces them to keep the memory of the previous partner alive for erotic purposes.

Abby   Who told you that?

Stu   Me. And it's true.

Abby   Only if you're a wanker.

Pause.

Stu   I suppose having a kid – you'd see the world again, wouldn't you?

Abby   So they say.

Stu (*shrugs*)   The sun, the moon, the trees. All the stuff we take for granted. You'd see it through the baby's eyes, like new.

Pause.

D'you think it'd do the same for us? D'you think we'd see each other again, like new?

Pause.

What would we call it?

Abby   If we had it?

He shrugs: obviously.

I like Rachel – or Amy's nice –

Stu   If it's a girl . . .

Abby   I know it sounds weird – but I get the feeling it is.

Stu   What if it's not?

Abby   If it's a boy? I quite like Rupert . . .

Stu   No way – Rupert??

Abby   Just because it was my grandad's name. Or there's Daniel – I like Daniel.

Stu   Daniel. Danny.

Pause.

Better than Rupert, anyway.

Pause.

Abby   Stuart – what are you saying here?

Stu   What am I saying?

Pause.

I'm saying I don't think we're done yet. It feels like there's more; like there's further we have to go. Doesn't it feel like that to you?

Pause.

Abby   I don't know. There's been so much hurt and pain . . .

Stu   But that's what I mean; what was it all for? If it ends here – if this is that's-it – then we went through all that hurt and pain for nothing.

Pause.

Do you think we should have this kid? Is that what you want?

Pause.

Abby   Yes. It's what I want. God knows why, but I do. But I need you to want it too.

Pause.

Stu   Oh, go on then.

Abby   'Go on then?'

Stu   Hey: our parents were fucked. Look how normal we turned out.

Pause.

So fuck it. Let's do it.

Abby   Stuart – are you sure about this? Because you can't be changing your mind on this every day. I can't take it, I really can't.

Pause. He really thinks about it.

Stu   Look, Abby, I love you. I don't want to love anyone else.
It's too fucking tiring.

Pause.

I want you to be the last person I love.

Pause. She goes to him, embraces him.

Abby   You know you can be quite romantic in your own twisted perverse fucked-up way.

Stu   I love it when you talk dirty to me.

Music.

They kiss: a long, passionate kiss – the way people who can't escape each other do.

Then they dance, the way people who can't dance do: laughing, happy.

The music ends abruptly. They separate.

And **Abby** *notices something.*

Abby   Look: it got dark.

Lightning Source UK Ltd.
Milton Keynes UK
03 July 2010

156480UK00001B/57/P

9 780413 772930